FunTime® Piano

LEVEL 3A - 3B

Arranged by Nancy and Randall Faber

This book belongs to: _____

Production Coordinator: Jon Ophoff
Editor: Isabel Otero Bowen
Design and Illustration: Terpstra Design, San Francisco
Engraving: Dovetree Productions, Inc.

FABER
PIANO ADVENTURES®

HAL•LEONARD®

A NOTE TO TEACHERS

FunTime® Piano Disney brings together contemporary and classic Disney hits arranged for the Level 3A-3B pianist. In the words of Walt Disney, "There is more treasure in books than in all the pirates' loot on Treasure Island." This book offers musical treasure for piano students with blockbusters from *Beauty and the Beast, Coco, Frozen, Hercules, The Little Mermaid, Pocahontas,* and more.

FunTime® Piano is part of the PreTime to BigTime Supplementary Piano Library arranged by Faber & Faber. The series allows students to enjoy a favorite style at their current level of study.

FunTime books are available in the following styles: *Popular, Classics, Favorites, Rock 'n Roll, Jazz & Blues, Ragtime & Marches, Hymns, Kids' Songs, Christmas, Jewish Favorites, Hits,* and the *Faber Studio Collection.*

Visit us at **PianoAdventures.com**.

Helpful Hints:

1. The songs can be assigned in any order. Selection is usually best made by the student, according to interest and enthusiasm.

2. Hands-alone practice is often helpful. Ensure that the playing is rhythmic even in hands-alone practice.

3. As rhythm is of prime importance, encourage the student to feel the rhythm in his or her body when playing. This can be accomplished with the tapping of the toe or heel, and with clapping exercises.

THE PRETIME TO BIGTIME PIANO LIBRARY

PreTime® Piano	=	Primer Level
PlayTime® Piano	=	Level 1
ShowTime® Piano	=	Level 2A
ChordTime® Piano	=	Level 2B
FunTime® Piano	=	Level 3A–3B
BigTime® Piano	=	Level 4 & above

ISBN 978-1-61677-721-0

Printed in U.S.A.

TABLE OF CONTENTS

Ev'rybody Wants to Be a Cat

from THE ARISTOCATS

Words by FLOYD HUDDLESTON
Music by AL RINKER

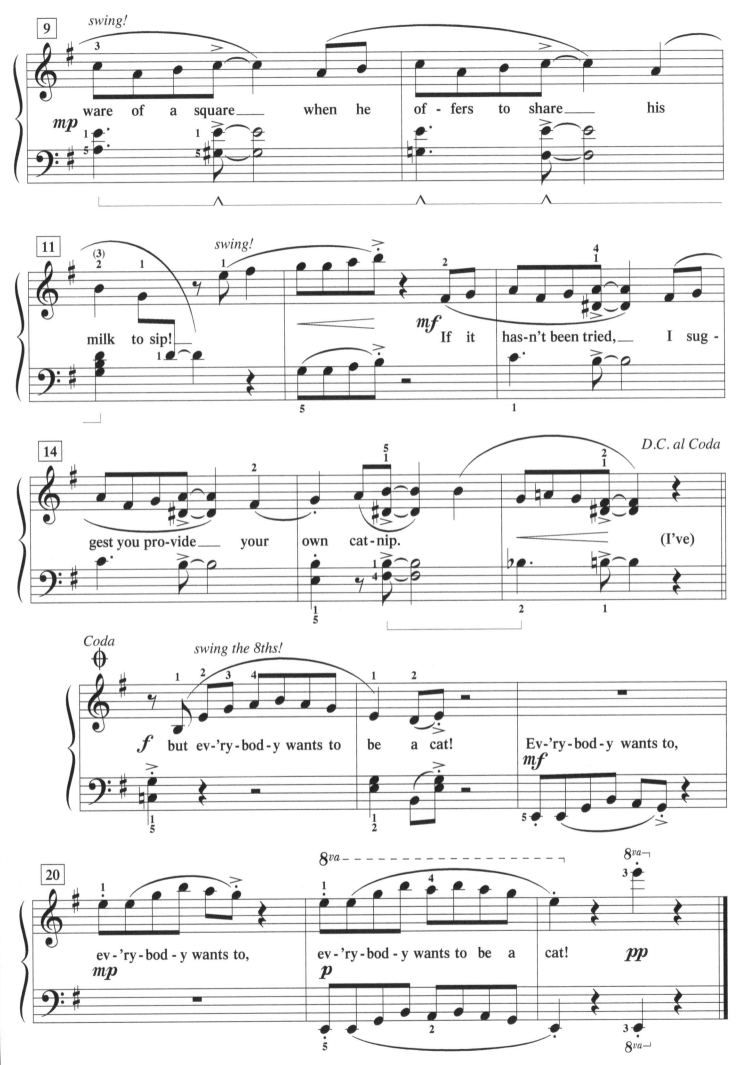

Cruella De Vil

from *101 DALMATIANS*

Words and Music by
MEL LEVEN

vam - pi - re bat,____ this in - hu - man beast,____ she

ought to be locked up____ and nev - er re - leased.____ The

world was such a whole - some place un - til Cru -

el - la, Cru - el - la De Vil.

Do You Want to Build a Snowman?

from *FROZEN*

Music and Lyrics by
KRISTEN ANDERSON-LOPEZ
and ROBERT LOPEZ

Be Our Guest

from *Beauty and the Beast*

Music by ALAN MENKEN
Lyrics by HOWARD ASHMAN

Remember Me
(Ernesto de la Cruz)

from *Coco*

Words and Music by
KRISTEN ANDERSON-LOPEZ
and ROBERT LOPEZ

Slowly, with expression

Colors of the Wind

from *POCAHONTAS*

Music by ALAN MENKEN
Lyrics by STEPHEN SCHWARTZ

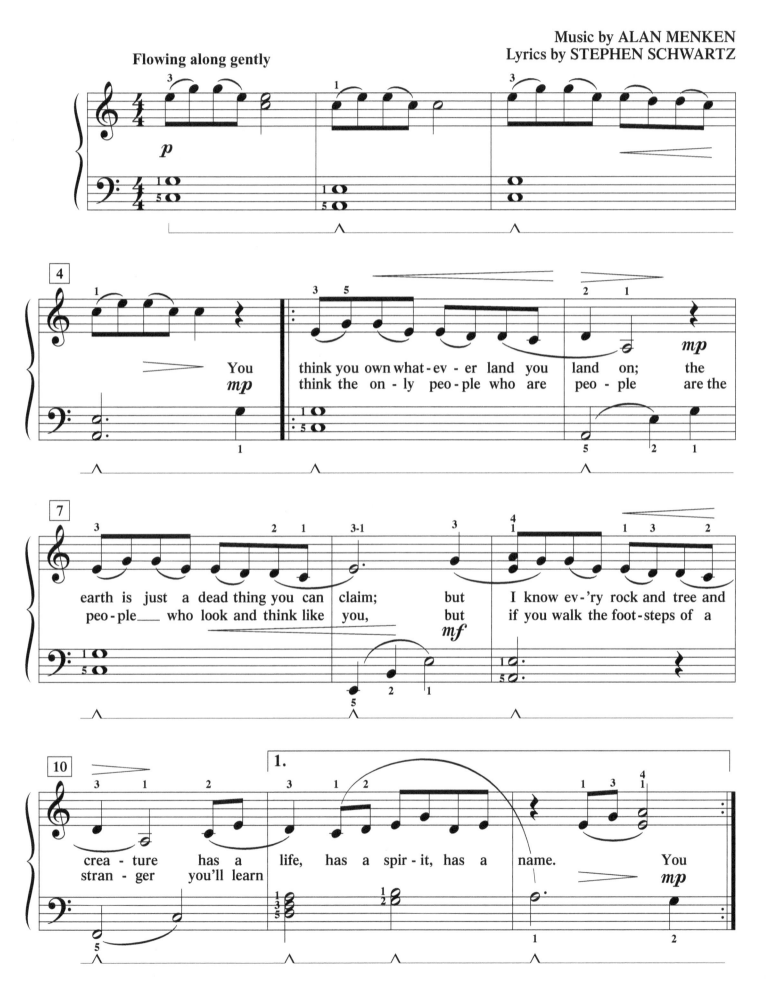

18

God Bless Us Everyone

from *A Christmas Carol*

Words and Music by ALAN SILVESTRI
and GLEN BALLARD

FF3054

20

pray. A mir - a - cle has just be -

broaden

gun;

f God bless us, ev - ry

a tempo

one.

rit.

a tempo
mf

cresc.

rit.

ff

L.H.

FF3054

Under the Sea

from *THE LITTLE MERMAID*

Music by ALAN MENKEN
Lyrics by HOWARD ASHMAN

sea. Dar - lin', it's bet - ter down where it's wet - ter. Take it from me. Up on the shore they work all day. Out in the sun they slave a - way, while we de - vo - tin' full time to float - in' un - der the sea.

(prepare)

When She Loved Me

from *TOY STORY 2*

Music and Lyrics by
RANDY NEWMAN

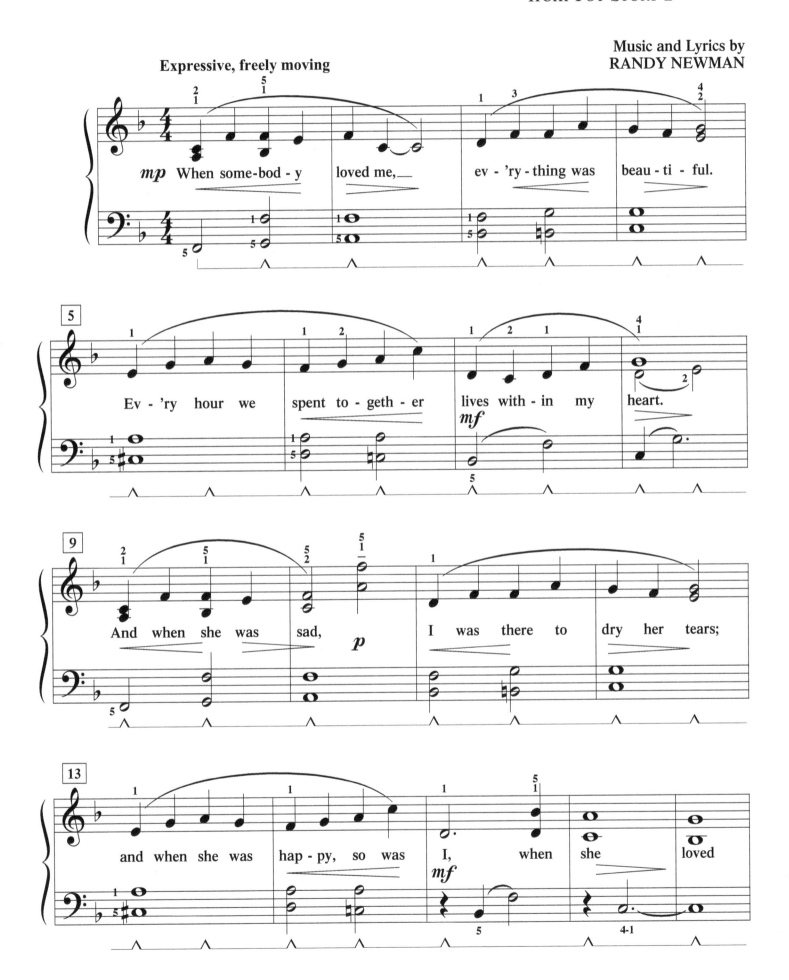

Go the Distance

from *HERCULES*

Music by ALAN MENKEN
Lyrics by DAVID ZIPPEL

look be-yond___ the glo-ry is the hard-est part,___ for a___

he - ro's strength is meas - ured by his heart.

L.H. over

rit. Like a shoot - ing star,___

a tempo

Zero to Hero

from *HERCULES*

Music by ALAN MENKEN
Lyrics by DAVID ZIPPEL